THREE stories. Three Brownie friends.
Three exciting trips together.
That's what this journey has for you!
The Brownie friends travel the world and
meet many girls. Through their stories,
you'll meet these girls, too.

A World of Girls

Girl Scouts of the USA

FLIP your book over!
On the other side, you'll have
loads of fun as you find stories,
tell stories, and change stories, too.

Chair,
National Board
of Directors

Connie L. Lindsey

Chief
Executive
Officer

Kathy Cloninger

Chief
Operating
Officer

Jan Verhage

Vice
President,
Program

Eileen Doyle

girl scouts

the dove
self-esteem
fund

Photographs

Side A: Page 13: The Royal Hashemite Court; **Page 23:** Courtesy of belovedqueen.com; **Page 38:** Michael Nichols/Getty Images; **Side B: Page 14:** Courtesy of Arhoolie Productions Inc.; **Page 19:** Makiko Hoh; **Page 23 and 28:** Lesley Williams

Illustration

Side B: Page 22: Used with permission by Emily Arnold McCully and Farrar, Straus and Giroux Publishing

Text printed on Fedrigoni Cento 40 percent de-inked, post-consumer fibers and 60 percent secondary recycled fibers.

Covers printed on Prisma artboard FSC Certified mixed sources.

This publication was made possible by a generous grant from the Dove Self-Esteem Fund.

WRITTEN BY Anne Marie Welsh, Laura J. Tuchman, Andrea Bastiani Archibald, Valerie Takahama, and Frankie Wright

ILLUSTRATED BY Helena Garcia

DESIGNED BY Sara Gillingham for Charette Communication Design

EXECUTIVE EDITOR: Laura J. Tuchman

ART AND PRODUCTION: Douglas Bantz, Ellen Kelliher, Sarah Micklem, Sheryl O'Connell, Lesley Williams

© 2010 by Girl Scouts of the USA

First published in 2010 by Girl Scouts of the USA
420 Fifth Avenue, New York, NY 10018-2798

www.girlscouts.org

ISBN: 978-0-88441-750-7

Printed in Italy

2 3 4 5 6 7 8 9/18 17 16 15 14 13 12 11

Contents

WELCOME TO
A World

"ONCE UPON A TIME . . ."

Those words always let you know that a story is about to start. As you turn these pages, you'll find amazing stories about three Brownie friends. Learning about others in faraway places and close to home, and listening to their stories and sharing your own—what a great way to learn about the wide World of Girls!

As you learn about girls all around the world, you'll learn all about yourself, too. You'll see just how much you can do!

You have the power to make the world better—for you *and* girls all around the world. That's something to be proud of. And it's a story you'll want to share, with everyone, everywhere!

# of Girls

BUT
FIRST,
the
First
Brownie
Story

Girl Scouts have always loved stories. They like to tell stories, and they like to do things that make good stories.

Even the name "Brownies" comes from a story. Brownies were elves who did good deeds while people slept. Like fairies, they were tiny, and people usually didn't see them.

In one famous old story, a brownie asks children to do good deeds on their own. That way people wouldn't need the magic of brownies during the night.

The Girl Scouts made that story their own. Now Brownie Elf and Grandmother Elf encourage ordinary girls to do extraordinary things. If you haven't already met Brownie Elf and Grandmother Elf, you'll meet them very soon!

Flying into Shali's Desert Home

Brownie friends Campbell, Jamila, and Alejandra played in the sunshine in the park in their hometown of Green Falls. Jam and Ali—those were their nicknames— sang Campbell's new jump-rope song. It went like this:

I know two elves from Scotland
who want every girl to be

just as happy, strong, and friendly
as Ali, Jam, and me!

The girls jump-roped to the song over and over. Alejandra finally stopped to catch her breath. "Campbell, it's time for a song with *your* name in it," she said.

"Didn't you say that your name is Scottish?" Jamila asked. "What are girls like in Scotland? Do you think they sing jump rope songs?"

Campbell laughed. "Yes, my name is Scottish. But I don't really know much about Scotland."

Alejandra grinned. "I know who does!" she said

"Me, too!" said Jamila. Then they all raised their arms, jiggled their bracelets, and called out:

Twist me and turn me and show me the elf.
I looked in the mirror and saw . . . myself.

Twist Me and Turn Me . . .

"Twist me and turn me and show me the elf. I looked in the water and saw _____."

Those words with the fill-in-the-blank at the end are part of the earliest Girl Scout Brownie story—and of every Brownie story since. Brownies who are all grown up still remember those beloved lines. When you're older, you may find yourself remembering them, too!

Poof! Their good friend, Brownie Elf, appeared. "Scotland?" she asked. "You know a lot about Scotland!"

But the girls were startled. Their friend stood in the doorway of something very strange.

"What is *that*?" Campbell pointed to the big, colorful *thing* behind Brownie Elf. It was sleek and silvery but all puffed up. Was it a giant, silver balloon? No! It had red wheels and a purple door, and yellow skis underneath. To top it off, there was a cherry-red chimney and a big white umbrella that shaded the roof!

"Is it a giant banana split?" Alejandra giggled.

"A rocket?" asked Jamila.

Grandmother Elf popped her head out the door. "It's my *bookmobile!* It's full of books. I zip all over the world in it, taking books to girls. In Scotland, I'm a librarian, you know."

The girls ran to greet their visitors. Grandmother Elf brought out a tray with a teapot and a plate of cookies. "Care for tea and biscuits?" she asked.

"*Biscuits,* those are cookies in Scotland!" Jamila said.

"And Scottish girls are called *lasses*," Campbell said.

"Ah, you *do* know something about Scotland," said Brownie Elf. "What about other countries? Would you like to meet other girls in places far, far away?"

The girls all talked at once. "Oh, yes!" "The world?" "The whole world?" "Where will we go?"

Campbell jumped up. "The library!" she yelled. They didn't have to go far! Grandmother Elf's bookmobile was filled with books. Laptops and electronic reading screens were in every corner. There were comfy chairs and tables, too. The walls were hung with photos of girls from all around the world.

The Brownie friends opened one book after another. They used the computers to search for more books. Jamila found one about a faraway land called Jordan. "It has cities, deserts—and girls like us," she said. They all leaned in to look. Then they nodded their heads. "Yes!"

WORDS WORTH KNOWING

SPIRES are like spears. They're towers that point up. **DOMES** are rounded towers on the roof of a building. They can be as round as the top of your head!

Poof! The big white umbrella popped up higher and the bookmobile rose toward the clouds. Suddenly, the girls felt little bulges in their jacket pockets. They reached in and pulled out small, slim notebooks. Campbell's was red, Jamila's was purple, Alejandra's was yellow. "Those are your passports," Grandma Elf said. "Fill them with everything you see and do as we travel!"

And so, their adventure had begun! The girls pressed their faces against the windows of the bookmobile. They saw blue sky above and sandy-colored hills below. Soon they spotted skyscrapers and glittering **domes** and **spires**. Trees and gardens, and buildings old and new, spread over many hills.

The bookmobile was hovering over the desert city of Amman, in the country of Jordan. Soon it landed in a small park next to a tall apartment building. A girl came skipping out its front door.

Brownie Elf called to her, "Hi, Shali! Peace."

"Salaam!" Shali said, which sounded like *zah-LAM*. "And peace be with you, too. Wow, look at this . . . whatever it is!"

Jamila smiled. "It's a bookmobile. It's for taking books to people who don't live near a library. We didn't know what it was at first, either," she said.

After all the girls said hello, Shali told them she and her mother were going to pick figs on her cousins' farm.

"Let us take you," said Grandmother Elf.

In a blink, the whole group was traveling along a dusty road outside the city. Brownie Elf steered the bookmobile while Grandmother Elf showed the girls books about Jordan. One book told about Jordan's queen, Queen Rania.

When the bookmobile stopped, Shali's cousins greeted them. They said *Marhaba,* which sounds like *MAR-ha-ba* and means *hello* in Arabic.

Jamila and Alejandra walked toward a grove of fig trees with Shali's cousins, who led two donkeys alongside them. Each donkey had empty baskets on its back. Brownie Elf drove the bookmobile behind them.

A Caring Queen

QUEEN RANIA of Jordan has her own video channel on the Internet, where she answers questions about her country. She even made a music video to inspire the world to end poverty.

Queen Rania cares about schoolchildren and works to get more computers in Jordan's schools. She also cares about girls and women. She wants them to have better lives, in Jordan and all around the world.

"Reading is important," said Grandmother Elf. "Maybe we can find some books that are just right for you. What do you like to read about?"

"Plants," said Shali. "I have lots of books at home, but most have big words and I can't figure them out."

"I trip up on words that aren't even big!" Campbell said. "But Jam and Ali help me out."

"*Girls teaching girls*," said Grandmother Elf. "That's what I like to see!"

Campbell laughed. "That sounds like a jump-rope song!" she said. And then she made one up.

Girls teaching girls—that's what I like to see. Shali picked some figs today, tomorrow Shali reads!

"That's great," Shali said. "Let's sing it to my cousins." As everyone picked figs from the fig trees, they sang the song and put in a new girl's name each time.

Soon their baskets were full, and
Shali's cousins tied them onto the donkeys to
carry home. Shali's mother turned to the girls. "Did
you taste a fig?" she asked. "Try one." The girls had never
seen a fig before. What a sweet surprise!

When they reached her cousins' home, Shali invited the girls
to play table tennis.

"We call it 'ping-pong,'" said Jamila. "Different name, same game!"

Shali showed the girls the best places to stand behind the table to hit
the ball. Then, wham! Jamila served.

"Great shot, Jam!"

"Now you try it, Ali!"

Whee! The ball flew by.

"Try bouncing it, like this," Shali said. She darted from
side to side, turning her wrist left and right so
the paddle smacked the ball just right.

The girls took turns playing. Soon Shali's
mother carried out a tray with sweet,
chilled tea in glasses with silver handles.
Mint leaves swirled inside them.

Inside the bookmobile, Shali and Campbell talked with Grandmother Elf. "More than anything, I want to be a good reader," Shali said.

"Tea. What a nice link to people all around the world," said Brownie Elf. She winked at Grandmother Elf.

"I wonder where else in the world people drink tea and like to read books?" Jamila asked.

Alejandra said, "I know where we can find out."

"The bookmobile!" said Campbell.

As they rode the bookmobile back to Shali's home in the city of Amman, Grandmother Elf and the girls looked through more books. Before long, they reached Shali's apartment.

Shali and her mother gave each girl some figs as a gift. They said *Ma'assalama*, which sounded like *MAH ah-sah-LAY-mah* and means *good-bye*.

"*Ma'assalama*," the girls repeated.

Then *poof!* Off they went.

Stories on the Go

The first American bookmobile was a horse-drawn carriage. That was in 1905. Later, librarians used mules and horses to bring books into the mountains. To reach islands, they used rowboats. Buses and campers are now bookmobiles, too! In Ethiopia, donkeys carry books. In Kenya, camels do. Imagine your own fantastic bookmobile! Draw it or build it!

Girls TEACHING Girls

Jamila and Alejandra are good readers, so they teach Campbell. Shali is so good at ping-pong that she showed her special moves to the Brownie friends. List the skills you have and use to teach friends new things. Then think of what your friends teach you! Skills can be passed back and forth, just like a ping-pong ball!

Skills I Share

piano
reading
drawing
making cards

Skills My Friends Share with Me

dancing
magic

Dancing with Chosita

The bookmobile landed on soft grass. The girls jumped out and saw bananas hanging from big green leaves. Butterflies fluttered among mango trees and papaya trees. Bright birds soared overhead. On the ground, scuttling and clucking, were dozens of chickens!

Grandmother Elf and Brownie Elf had flown the bookmobile all the way to Thailand.

"Look over there!" called Alejandra.

The Brownie friends saw a girl about their age. She was busy gathering eggs. When she saw the visitors, she nearly dropped all the eggs from her basket!

"Got it!" Campbell said, catching an egg just in time. She handed it to the girl and explained, "This is a bookmobile. It takes books all around the world!"

The girl smiled and said hello. Her name was Chosita, which means "happiness." Then she went back to gathering eggs. "I need to get these to the temple," she said. "The eggs are used to bake cakes for **ceremonies**." The girls joined in and soon all the eggs were nestled in Chosita's basket.

"*Khobkhun!*" said Chosita. That means "thank you" in Thai and it sounds like *kobe-kun*. "Would you like to come with me to the temple?" she asked.

"Let's go in the bookmobile!" Jamila said.

WORDS WORTH KNOWING

CEREMONIES are ways we honor a special time, like a birth or a wedding. When you were in kindergarten, did your class have a graduation at the end of the year? That was a ceremony! What Girl Scout ceremonies do you like most?

WORDS WORTH KNOWING

A **TYPHOON** is a huge storm with very strong winds and rain. In some parts of the world, a typhoon is called a **HURRICANE**.

"Really?" Chosita asked. "I love to read, but my school doesn't have many books. A **typhoon** hit and all the books got soaked!"

The Brownies listened as Chosita told them about the roaring winds and flooding waters. They told her about a **hurricane** that hit their country. "We all pitched in to get new books to libraries and schools," Campbell said. "I'll bet you and other girls here in Thailand can do something like that."

Grandmother Elf looked around the library. "And here is a whole shelf of books that may be just right for your school. They'll give you and your classmates something to read while you gather more books."

"Thank you!" Chosita said.

The bookmobile came to a gentle
stop. The girls could see the temple at
the top of a hill. People seemed to be moving
across the walls!

"They look like dancers," Jamila said. "Are they?"
As they all climbed the hill to the temple, Chosita
explained, "Those are very old carvings of temple dancers."
When they reached the temple, the girls saw that, sure enough,
dancers were carved into the stone walls. Some of the carvings
were damaged.

"These were hurt in the typhoon," Chosita said. "But this **frieze** still tells a very old story. I learned the dances for it. I'll show you!"

Chosita raised her arms and waved them softly, moving her hands as if telling a story with her fingers. The Brownie friends followed along, moving their hands from side to side just like Chosita.

"This is fun, but it's not easy," Campbell said.

"I practice every day!" Chosita said.

Chosita then took the eggs to the temple and soon returned with a beautiful lantern shaped like a lotus flower. "I brought this from the temple," she told the girls. "I wish you could stay to see our Floating Lantern Festival at the end of the rainy season."

Just then, Grandmother Elf came with a book of photographs of the festival. The pictures showed lights on every river and stream, like fireworks on the water.

A Musical Queen

QUEEN SIRIKIT and King Bhumibol have ruled Thailand for more than 50 years. Queen Sirikit likes to write songs. She also works for her country's Red Cross, which helps people after disasters such as typhoons and tidal waves. Queen Sirikit has been a queen longer than anyone else in the world!

"My family makes lots of lanterns for the festival," Chosita said. "I'd love for you to meet my family!"

And so they headed to Chosita's home in the bookmobile, past green fields of rice plants rippling in the breeze. "I work in the rice paddies with my family," Chosita said. She sang a rice-planting song, "Rhii rhii, khoa saan," which sounded like *Ree, ree, koh-a san*.

Chosita's house was built on thick poles like stilts. Chosita left her shoes by the steps. "Please come meet my mother," she said.

The girls, too, left their shoes by the stairs. Inside, in a big room, they saw colorful, shimmering fabrics.

"Thailand is famous for its silk," Chosita's mother said. She and Chosita's grandmother had woven the silk themselves. Some of it glittered with gold threads. The family made silks for the many children and grandchildren of the queen and king of Thailand.

"How about I teach you my favorite game?" Chosita asked. "It's called *Ling Ching Lak*, or Monkey Fighting for the Poles. It's one of the oldest games in the world."

Chosita explained the game and Campbell agreed to be the monkey. The other girls stood by one of three big trees in Chosita's yard. Those trees were "safe."

"Ready, set . . . go!" shouted Campbell.

When the "monkey" gave the signal, the girls took off, each trying to reach a tree before the monkey caught them. A girl with no tree became "it."

Alejandra laughed. "Oops! Now I'm the monkey! Ready, set, go!"

"I like this game," Jamila said. "It reminds me of our games of tag and musical chairs."

After the girls played, they ate mango slices and sipped spiced tea under the shade of a banyan tree.

Then it was time for Chosita and her mother to join the rest of their family in the rice paddies. They gave each girl a square of silk—purple for Jamila, red for Campbell, yellow for Alejandra. The girls said thank you and Chosita and her mother waved good-bye.

"There are so many girls in the world. Who will we visit next?" Alejandra asked.

"We've been to warm countries so far," Jamila said.

"How about someplace cold?" asked Grandmother Elf. "I know the perfect place to get cozy with new friends and a good story—and some nice hot tea!"

"Hooray!" shouted the girls.

And then *poof!* Off they went!

WORDS WORTH KNOWING

HEROINES are women or girls who act with special courage—in real life or in stories.

GIRLS FOREVER!

In Thailand, all schoolchildren wear uniforms. And each day, they place their lunches in the middle of the table and share their food.

หญิงสาว means "girl" in Thai, the language of Thailand. It sounds like *say-ow*.

Some girls take part in making silk, too. They feed mulberry leaves to silkworms, which look like caterpillars. When the silkworms spin their cocoons, the girls gather them and learn to turn their silk threads into yarn, and then into cloth.

Some girls in Thailand work on their family's farm. They plant and gather rice from the fields, feed and tend animals, and collect eggs.

Favorite Girls

What are your favorite girl characters like? Are they brave? Are they strong? Are they **heroines**? What do they do to make the world better?

Name your favorite characters and what you like best about them. Then fill in what's best about being you! You can add to this list for a long time!

What's best about my favorite girl characters	What's best about me
Are nice	generous
brave	kind
strong	creative
talented	friendly
heroines	funny

Story Swapping with Lakti

As the wheels came up and big, shiny yellow skis dropped down, the bookmobile glided across the ice. The girls had arrived in the Arctic region of Canada. They were bundled up in parkas, earmuffs, boots, and mittens.

Campbell looked out the window. "Look! Reindeer!"

The bookmobile stopped. A girl carrying a pail ran to greet them. "Hello, Lakti," Grandmother Elf said. "Meet my friends, Jamila, Alejandra, and Campbell."

The Brownie girls peeked into Lakti's pail as she named what was inside: "Mussels, sea urchins, and two kinds of fish—arctic char and whitefish." The girls stared into the pail, but Lakti's eyes were on the bookmobile.

Lakti and her family and friends knew many stories. They were members of the Ungava Inuit, a group of native people from far up in eastern Canada. Ungava means "toward the open water."

"The Inuit know so many stories, we sometimes have trouble remembering all of them," Lakti said. "We would love to record them. Maybe we could put them in a bookmobile!"

"I have ways to help you do that," Grandmother Elf said. "After all, hearing stories from long ago is so much fun. Those stories are your very own **folktales**!"

WORDS WORTH KNOWING

FOLKTALES are made-up stories passed on from generation to generation. Folktales are often told out loud. "Little Red Riding Hood" is a folktale.

Lakti's great aunt was a storyteller. Every week, villagers gathered to hear her tales. The stories she told were passed down to her by older storytellers. And those older storytellers heard them from even older storytellers. Some stories were about things that happened hundreds of years ago.

"Does she tell stories about sea creatures like the ones in your bucket?" Jamila asked.

"Sometimes," Lakti answered. "Before you meet her, do you want to see how we fish when the water in the bay is frozen?"

"Awesome!" said Alejandra.

Lakti explained that she lives on the shore of the Hudson Bay, which stays frozen all winter. She led them to a spot with a hole in the ice. The hole was the size of a small plate.

The air was icy cold. The girls clapped their hands as Lakti dropped her fishing line into the hole and jiggled it to catch the attention of a fish. "You have to watch carefully, so you don't miss when the fish bites," she said. "My friends and I swap stories to pass the time. Do you ever do that?"

Just then, Lakti felt a tug on her fishing line. She reeled it out of the hole and dropped a wriggling fish into her bucket.

"Hooray!" the girls shouted.

"Now you try," said Lakti.

Time flew by as the girls talked and pulled in three more fish. Before they knew it, Lakti's bucket was full.

Paddles and Skis

The Ungava Inuit have been kayakers for hundreds of years. They love to paddle from island to island in the summer. In winter, they use skis and snowmobiles to get around.

Fluffy Berry Akutaq

Families once took *akutaq* with them when they traveled and hunted. Now it is eaten as a dessert, a school snack, or as a spread on crackers or bread. Families often form *akutaq* into fun shapes, like balls or little seals, and freeze them before eating.

"Now, let's go see my great aunt," Lakti said.

The girls took turns carrying the bucket as they hurried to Lakti's house on the shore.

Grandmother Elf greeted them. "How about a hot drink? Some tea, perhaps? Or hot cocoa?"

Lakti smiled. "And some **akutaq**!"

Campbell repeated the word exactly as Lakti had said it. "What's *a-koo-tak*?"

"It's our ice cream," Lakti answered. "It's sweet and fluffy, with berries. You'll love it!"

Cups of hot cocoa warmed the girls' hands. As they sipped, Lakti took out all the makings for *akutaq*.

"*Akutaq* means 'mix them together' in our Yupik language," she explained. "Every family has its own recipe. Ours uses boiled fish and sugar and lots of berries—blueberries, blackberries, and cranberries."

The girls mixed everything together.

When everyone had their fill of the fluffy treat, Lakti invited them to meet her Great Aunt Mary. The girls brought Mary a bowl of *akutaq*. They all settled in a half-circle around her.

"Once, when I was about Lakti's age, my great grandmother handed me a beautiful piece of green stone," she said. "It was time for me to learn to carve."

Mary talked about the tools and the art of carving, and how each carver sees a shape in the stone. "In our village, we can just look at a carving and tell who made it," Lakti added. "Each artist has her own **style**!"

Lakti and her great aunt showed the girls small carvings of girls, and mothers with children.

"I want to carve a baby riding in the hood of her mother's parka," she said. "That will take time."

33

"And patience," said Campbell, "just like fishing!"

"Or like anything else you want to do well," said Aunt Mary, "even telling stories."

Then Lakti remembered! "Aunt Mary, Grandmother Elf has new ways for us to keep our stories." Great Aunt Mary smiled.

"Everything's in the bookmobile," Grandmother Elf said. "Let's go!" Once in the bookmobile, Grandmother Elf pulled out a camera, a video camera, and a laptop.

"There are so many ways to tell stories," she said. "You don't always have to write them down. You can take photos or make sketches, or use a video camera."

She handed Lakti some notebooks, the cameras, and the laptop. "Sometimes it's good to have stories saved in more than one way—in a notebook, on a video, or in a computer file. Then if one gets lost or damaged, you and your friends will still have another copy of the story!"

Lakti thanked everyone. Aunt Mary gave each girl a tiny stone carving of a fish as a souvenir of their visit.

"I hope we can come back to fish again with you someday," Alejandra said.

Lakti and her great aunt smiled. "We hope so, too," Lakti said, and she waved good-bye.

Brownie Elf turned to the girls, "Let's get you home so you can tell stories of your adventures in this wide world of girls."

The girls settled into the bookmobile, and *poof!* Before they knew it, they were back in the park in their hometown of Green Falls. They stood in the sunshine in the same clothes they had on before they left. Their parkas were gone.

Jamila picked up the jump rope they'd left behind before their adventures. "Let's finish our jump rope song!" she said.

The girls huddled together and then started singing.

In Jordan, we met Shali—and all her cousins, too! Her reading got much better and we saw what girls could do!

Chosita showed us Thailand. We tried a brand-new dance. We brought new books for children so they'll have a better chance.

We met Lakti in the Arctic. She had so many tales to share. She will save her auntie's stories with the tools that we brought there!

"That was good," said Jamila. "Let's keep going."
"You're good storytellers!" Grandmother Elf said.
"Meeting girls around the world inspired you!"
"That's right," Brownie Elf said. "And now, Grandmother and I must be going."

"Just one more verse, please?" Campbell asked.
Together the girls sang a final rhyme:

Our special friends from Scotland, a world of girls they've shown.
Now we can make things better with great stories of our own!

They stopped jumping and turned to say thank you.
Brownie Elf and her grandmother smiled. Then *poof!*
They and the bookmobile were gone, just like that.

"I can't wait to draw pictures that tell stories of all we did!" Alejandra said.

"Remember how Chosita danced that old story?" asked Jamila. "I'm going to dance new stories for girls everywhere!"

"I'll build a bookmobile to hold your stories," Campbell said.

The girls laughed. Then, their passports safe in their pockets, they headed home.

Storytelling Spots

All over the world, women gather around campfires, near water wells, on the banks of rivers, and in other special places to share stories. Where do the women in your family gather to share stories?

GIRLS FOREVER!

In Canada, many Inuit live in Nunavut, which means "Our Land." Parts of Nunavut are close to the North Pole and as far north as humans live on planet Earth.

"*Niviasar*" is how you say *girl* in the Inuktitut language. The word sounds like *ni-Vy-a-sar*.

Susan Aglukark is a famous Inuit singer and songwriter. She records pop songs that tell Inuit stories.

This is how Susan's name looks in her native language, Inuktitut:

ᐊᒡᓗᑲᖅ

Stories Are Keepsakes, Keepsakes Tell Stories!

Has a woman in your life ever told you a story about when she was younger? Has she given you something she cherished as a girl, like a favorite doll? Did she tell you a story about it? Draw or paste a picture of something special to you. Then share a little story about this special thing.

A World of Girls

Girl Scouts of the USA

FLIP this book over anytime you like.
Great stories, and great clues,
await you there, too!

STORIES hold clues to making the world
a better place. You are on a journey
to find those clues!

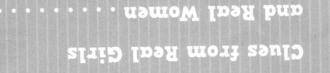

Contents

First, Your PASSPORT

A passport is like a ticket. It lets you go places you want to go, and it tells the story of your travels. If you've ever traveled outside your home country, you probably have a passport.

A World of Girls has a passport, too. Along this journey, your passport will tell the story of all you do as a leader, on your own and with your Brownie team.

Look at the next page and pages 38–40! Your passport will tell the wonderful story of your *A World of Girls* journey. So get started. Place a picture of yourself in your passport. Fill in other things about yourself, now or anytime you like.

MY PASSPORT

Photo here

Me! Melinda Pan

When and where I was born August 5th 2004 in USA

Where I live 196 Aster Dr. VHP

My Brownie group and where it meets
1142, Manor Oaks

Some important people in my life My family.
1142, Manor Oaks

My favorite color pink.

My favorite foods pizza.

Some special skills of mine piano.

Fun things I like to share with my friends
secrets.

The World Is FILLED with Girls, and Stories, Too!

Stories are everywhere, and so are girls! They're in books and movies. They're on the Web and on TV. Stories and girls are all over the world. They're all around you, too.

Stories are one of the best ways to explore what life is like for girls around the world. And in stories, you can find clues about what you might do to make life better for girls, near and far!

Making the world better for girls—that's the story of this journey. And that's the story of Girl Scouts, too! What a wonderful story!

Good stories have lots of action. One thing happens, then something else happens, and then something else! You're at the start of your journey story! What will happen next?

4 AWARDS, Just for You!

Awards are a beloved Girl Scout tradition! On this journey, as you explore stories and their clues, you'll earn important awards. When you add your awards to your Brownie vest, you'll feel proud and confident!

Your awards will remind you of all the fun you have on this journey. They will remind you of how you

Hear a Story

Change a Story

and Tell a Story.

And all together, they will remind you of how you made a change toward a

Better World for Girls!

Your awards will remind you of how you've grown as a leader who teaches and inspires others and makes the world a better place. Your awards will also remind you of the **story** of your journey. By sharing the story of your journey, you can inspire others to make the world better, too.

Stories and Their Clues

Everyone in your life has stories to share. So listen for stories wherever you go! When you hear a story, listen for clues about what could change to make things better. Maybe you can make those changes! And if you share the story, other people can join you in making those changes, too!

Daisy's World of Girls

Juliette "Daisy" Gordon Low started the Girl Scouts nearly 100 years ago. If Daisy were telling a story about herself when she was a girl, it would probably take place at her home in Georgia. Imagine what Daisy would have wanted to change in her world of girls!

A WORLD of GIRLS! How Do You Say GIRL in DUTCH?

ASK AROUND! WRITE IT HERE!

Finding a Good clue

Here's a story you probably know that has a clue in it: *Once there was a girl named Little Red Riding Hood. She walked alone through the forest to visit her grandmother, and on the way, she met a hungry wolf.*

Whoa! Walking alone through a forest is not safe! That's a clue. Little Red Riding Hood needs a safe way to get to her grandmother's house. That would change her life for the better, wouldn't it?

Here are some good ways to find clues in other stories you might hear:

❋ **Look for what might change to help the main character.** *Is it something you and your Brownie team could help change for others, too?*

Making a change is taking action! That's what this journey is all about. And that's what Girl Scouts is all about. Taking action can change a story for the better.

ASK AROUND! WRITE IT HERE!

A WORLD of GIRLS! How Do You Say GIRL in RUSSIAN?

CHANGING STORIES
for the Better

How about using clues to change stories for the better right now? Start with the adventures of the Brownie friends. Flip your book and take a look. What do you think needs to change for the better on their first adventure?

CLUE In Jordan, the Brownie friends meet Shali, who has trouble reading. She wants to read about plants, but books about them are too hard for her.

What I would change to make Shali's world better:

_____ .

This would make things better because:

_____ .

CLUE The books at Chosita's school in Thailand were ruined by a big storm.

What if you went to school and all the books there were damaged, too? What could you and your friends do about it?

_____

Now, try two more stories! What you would change in the following stories to make the characters' lives better? Don't know the stories? Visit a library!

Ramona Quimby, Age 8 by Beverly Cleary

CLUE Ramona gets goopy egg in her hair and thinks her teacher doesn't like her.

I would change_____.

This would make things better because: _____.

The Paperbag Princess by Robert Munsch

CLUE A girl faces the dragon who burned her clothes and decides to live her own life instead of marrying a prince.

I would change _____.

This would make things better because: _____.

Now, FIND A CLUE in Your Favorite Story

What is your favorite story that . . .

has main characters who are girls or women? _____.

has a clue that shows that something in the story needs to change for the better? _____.

How could you make the same kind of change in your world?

_____.

Clues CLOSE to HOME

The world's a big place, that's for sure! So you might get started listening for stories and their clues in your own girl world. Getting others to share their stories is a great way to learn about what the world needs.

When you ask someone to tell you a story, **BE PREPARED**. Have a few questions ready. Ask them what they remember about being a young girl.

Then ask these three questions:

1. *When you were younger, what did you want to change in the world?*

2. *What do you want to change about the world today?*

3. *What could my Brownie team and I do to bring about the change you want?*

If more questions come to mind, ask them as you go!

NOW, GIVE IT A TRY!

Picturing Your World of Girls

You've probably heard someone say, "A picture is worth a thousand words." That's because pictures can tell stories. Here's a place for pictures of the girls and women in your world! See if you can show what makes each girl or woman special to you.

Women in MY WORLD:
What They Want to Change, and
How I COULD MAKE That Change . . .

_____

_____

_____

_____

_____

Tell Your Stories Again and Again!

It's fun to tell stories over and over. Retell a story you learned from a woman in your life. Retell it in a fun way—with words, pictures, photographs, or things you find lying around, like leaves or pieces of fabric!

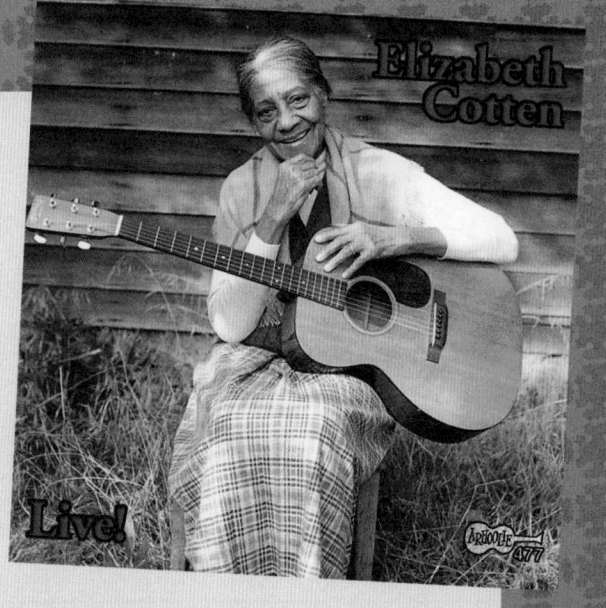

Elizabeth "Libba" Cotten

Live!

Elizabeth "Libba" Cotten was a guitar player who taught herself how to play guitar as a young girl. When she was 11, she bought her first guitar with money she saved. She named her guitar Stella.

Libba became famous for a song called "Freight Train," which she wrote when she was young. The song told the story of trains she saw coming and going from the University of North Carolina. Libba once said the story of how her song came to be was a long story. You can listen to her talk about the song and hear her sing it on the Web. Just ask an adult to find you a video of Libba playing "Freight Train."

> MUSIC IS A WAY TO SHARE STORIES, TOO!

STORIES CAN PLANT SEEDS OF UNDERSTANDING

Rhiana Yazzie writes plays, which are stories acted out on a stage. Rhiana believes plays can change the world.

Rhiana grew up in New Mexico. Her mother is Italian and black. Her father is a Navajo. So Rhiana tells stories that describe lots of places and lots of traditions. Her stories introduce us to new people and new cultures.

Her play, "Chile Pod," tells the story of Carmen, a girl who moved to the United States from Mexico. She speaks Mixtec, the Indian language of her homeland. Everyone else at her school speaks English or Spanish. So making friends is hard. But sharing music is easy. Carmen sees that music is a language everyone understands. By sharing her music, Carmen's life changes for the better.

What might you and your Brownie team do to make things better for new kids at school?

A WORLD of GIRLS! How do you say GIRL in SPANISH?
DO YOU KNOW? WRITE IT HERE!

Parks Make 🌳 the World BETTER!

Flip this book! Look at pages 6–7. The Brownie friends play together in a park in their hometown of Green Falls. Not all girls have such a nice place to play. So that's a story that needs to change! A nice, outdoor space to play in could make life better for some girls.

If you could create a park, what would it have? A skating rink? A big tree to read a story under? Water to drink or dip in? A garden? Birds? How would your park make girls' lives better? Draw your park here!

The Trefoil, the Girl Scout Symbol

The trefoil [pronounced TREH-foyl] has always been the Girl Scout symbol. It's the shape of the Girl Scout logo, too. See how the Girl Scout logo looks like three sisters? How about creating a symbol for another of your girl worlds?

Your BROWNIE World

An awesome thing about being a Girl Scout Brownie is that it gives you an instant world of girls! As you grow up in Girl Scouts, your connections to this world of girls keep on growing.

The Girl Scout Law says to be a sister to every Girl Scout. What would you do for your sister Brownies to make their world better?

So Many Worlds of Girls

You probably belong to many different girl worlds. Your Brownie group is one! You may play on a soccer team or belong to a gymnastics or dance group. If you ride a school bus, you may have a bus stop group. You might have a group of girls you eat lunch with, or some girl cousins you hang out with. All these groups are your girl worlds. Name them here:

My girl groups	What we do together
_____	_____
_____	_____
_____	_____
_____	_____
_____	_____

Food Can Remind You of a STORY . . .

In the flip side of this book, the Brownie friends visit Thailand. Lots of foods in Thailand mix sweet and spicy flavors. People there also mix salty foods with foods that are a little sour. Sound yummy? Try this dip from Thailand and see what you think. If you think it could be better, change it! Turn it into a story that you want to share!

Mango Dip

1   ripe mango, cut into chunks (ask an adult to cut it for you)

4   tablespoons coconut milk

1   teaspoon brown sugar

1   tablespoon fish sauce, or ¼ teaspoon salt

1   tablespoon lime juice

¼   teaspoon dried crushed chilies (like the red pepper put on pizza)

Mix everything together in a bowl, then chill the dip in a refrigerator for at least an hour. Bite-size pieces of cooked chicken or shrimp taste good dipped in this sauce, and so do chopped, fresh vegetables.

Make Your Own *Bento*

Read the story on the next page and then make your friends or your younger sister or brother a **bento**! Start by using your favorite cookie cutters to make little sandwiches in fun shapes, and to cut pieces of cheese and fruit into fun shapes, too.

A WORLD of GIRLS! How Do You Say GIRL in JAPANESE?

ASK AROUND! WRITE IT HERE!

Food that looks good usually tastes good. It invites you in, like a good story. "We eat with our eyes as much as with our taste buds and stomachs!" says **Makiko Itoh**. Do you agree?

Makiko likes to be called Maki for short. She was born in Japan and has lived all over the world. When she lived in England, she was a Brownie. Now she is an expert in making food look pretty. She likes to fill a special Japanese lunch box, called a *bento* box, with colorful food cut into fun shapes. Traditional *bento* boxes, called *obentos* in Japan, use a variety of foods—rice along with meat, fish, or egg, and lots of fruits and vegetables.

Maki loves sharing the *bento* story!

ALL OUR STUFF Has Stories!

Good stories, and good clues, can be found in all sorts of things. Hold a special stone in your hand or wear a favorite bracelet. Do these things remind you of a good feeling or a happy time? What stories might they tell?

In a way, all the things we own have a story to tell. Think of an umbrella going here and there, keeping you dry. Or a can opener saying, "Here comes the tuna. No. It's puppy food!" Or, "Ooh, peaches. Yum."

Now you try it! Here's some fun stuff. What might each thing say about what it sees every day?

" _____ "

" _____ "

" _____ "

Jumping for clues!

With your Brownie friends, have some fun thinking up a jump rope rhyme that tells a story with a clue. Start with . . .

One, two, we found a clue . . . .

Inventions Are STORIES That Change Things for the Better!

If you like to make things—and make things better—then you have plenty of stories to tell. In fact, a story in search of a better ending is what inventions are all about!

Think of it this way: Sometimes people see how things are and want to make them better. So they create something new. That's an invention!

Just think about the story of cell phones—people wanted to talk to one another any time, anywhere. The invention of the cell phone made that possible.

THE STORY OF THE REAL PAPERBAG PRINCESS!

Once upon a time, there lived a girl named **Margaret E. "Mattie" Knight**. She loved to make things. When she saw ways for a kite or a sled to work better, she built them. She even made a foot warmer to keep her grandmother's feet cozy.

Mattie's most famous gadget could cut and glue flat-bottomed paper bags. It's still used today, more than 130 years later!

When Mattie had an idea for a gadget, she drew it in a notebook and then made it. If you could invent a gadget that makes a change for the better, what would it be? Draw it in your notebook here.

Margaret E. "Mattie" Knight
as a young girl

A BOOK LOVER WITH AN EYE FOR CLUES

Madison Eve loves to read. "I was in kindergarten when I knew I loved reading books," she says. By the time she was 8 and in third grade, she had read all seven *Harry Potter* books.

In the sixth *Harry Potter* book, Madison discovered a clue that could have changed things for the better for her favorite character, Ginny Weasley. In the story, the evil Death Eaters destroy Ginny's house. "If she had asked others to help, she could have stopped them," Madison says.

Madison sometimes helps friends with their reading. "Kids will come up to me and ask what a word means. So I help them sound it out," she says.

A WORLD of GIRLS! How Do You Say GIRL in ITALIAN?

ASK AROUND! WRITE IT HERE!

Clues from Real Girls and Real Women

Sharing Is a Way to CHANGE THINGS for the Better

Being a reading buddy to a friend is a way to share your skills and talents. When you share what you know, you often learn new things, too. Sharing's a good thing to do with your Brownie friends, and with other people, too.

See if you can match the clues below with how to share to make things better.

CLUE

How I Can Share to Make Things Better

CLUE	How I Can Share to Make Things Better
Ana is sad because it's raining and she can't go to the beach.	See if she wants to sit under a tree, where it's cool.
Sofia is hungry because she forgot to bring her snack.	Ask if she'd like to draw a sand castle or build a castle out of blocks.
Kara is hot and tired.	Offer to give her half your orange.

TEAMING UP

Kiara Stephanie Woolfolk Ruiz is a Girl Guide. She lives in Ensenada, which is a town in Mexico near the Pacific Ocean. In Spanish, Girl Guides are called *guiás*. Kiara's favorite story is **Prince Caspian: The Return to Narnia**. In it, girls work together as a team. What Kiara really loves is that the girls don't give up. "When you are a young girl, you try to overcome all challenges." When girls work together toward one goal, Kiara says, "it's easier to succeed."

WINDOWS ON THE WORLD

Carolyn Marsden writes stories about places all around the world. She and her husband, Pal, who grew up in Thailand, have two daughters, Maleeka and Preeya. In school, Preeya was called "China" because her classmates thought she was Chinese. That led Carolyn to write a story called **The Gold-Threaded Dress**. In it, a Thai girl named Oy is teased for being different. Oy wants to be friends with the children who tease her but doesn't feel it is right to have to change herself. She learns that she can be accepted for who she is.

Carolyn has lots of ideas for stories. She thinks of them as "airplanes lined up on a runway, ready to take off." What story ideas do you have waiting on your runway?

A WORLD OF GIRLS! How do you say GIRL IN THAI?

ASK AROUND! WRITE IT HERE!

Words START Stories, Words BUILD Stories!

Read each sentence below to figure out which letters fit in the blanks. Then take the first letter of each word and put them together to spell a word that's special on this journey!

Red, green, and blue are examples of these.

▢ ___ ___ ___ ___ ___

It's where you can find lots of books—and lots of words!

▢ ___ ___ ___ ___ ___ ___

When something isn't right side up, it might be this.

▢ ___ ___ ___ ___ ___   ___ ___ ___ ___

This is what you do when you're hungry.

▢ ___ ___

You can tell them, and use them to make the world a better place!

▢ ___ ___ ___ ___ ___ ___

26

How to Make the Change YOU Want to See

As you hear a story and use its clue to make a change for the better, ***think about one girl in your community and how her life will be better because of what you are about to do.*** And then follow the steps and tips on this checklist:

☐ **Find a clue you care enough to act on.** *How? Look all around. A clue can be something small, but it will make things better.*

☐ **Make a team decision.** *How? Speak up. Listen to what everyone has to say. Then work together and agree on something most of your Brownie team wants to do.*

☐ **Plan.** *How? Use your Planning Sheet to figure out the steps, and then decide who will do what. Get some help from others!*

☐ **Carry out your plan!** *How? Make sure each of your Brownie teammates has something to do.*

A WORLD OF GIRLS! How do you say GIRL in SWEDISH?

ASK AROUND! WRITE IT HERE!

Reading was always easy for **Adele Ann Taylor**. But it wasn't easy for all of her classmates. Adele wanted to change that story! So when she was 13, she created Adele's Literacy Library (www.adelesliteracylibrary.org). *Literacy* means knowing how to read and write. Adele wanted her literacy library to give all people the chance to enjoy good books.

What Adele likes best about reading is that it lets her use her imagination. "When you read, you can go anywhere in the world," Adele says. "With reading, all things are possible."

Reaching Out in a Small Way Is Important!

"Mighty oaks from tiny acorns grow." What does this old saying mean? It means that much bigger, greater things can grow from something as small as a seed! So what you and your Brownie friends do together doesn't have to be a big thing. A small thing can be important, too!

How do you say GIRL in ARABIC? A WORLD OF GIRLS!

ASK AROUND! WRITE IT HERE

Little Stories
ALL AROUND YOU

You've probably seen advertisements on television and at the movies. Maybe you've heard them on the radio, too. Advertisements, also called ads, are little stories that try to sell you things.

Look—and listen—around you for a day or two for ads that have girls in them. Keep track of them here. Then talk with your Brownie friends about what you've found and what you might like to change about the ads.

Where I Saw the Ad	What the Ad Sells	Do the Girls in the Ad Look Like Me?
1		
2		
3		

Changing the World Means Telling a New Story

When you change the world a little or a lot, you get to tell a new story! And your story will have important clues in it—clues that show that you have the power to make changes for the better! That's important! The more people you share your clues with, the more people can get changes going. That means more things can change for the better. And that's the Girl Scout story: making changes to make the world a better place!

So whenever you create some change, be sure to tell the story of that change. Storytelling is loads of fun.

Just think of all the ways you have heard stories and can tell stories. Books, movies, cartoons, songs, dances, pictures, and games all tell stories.

Think about who needs to hear your story. Who will care the most about it? You've started a change. Who will keep it going? The people interested in your story may be younger than you, your age, or older than you. You could tell your story to a whole classroom full of people or you could tell it to just a few people. You could even tell your story to people you don't yet know. It's fun to meet new people—they can join you in making a change for the better!

How Will You Tell Your Story?

Once you know your story and your audience, you and your Brownie team can get creative in how you tell your story. You might . . .

* write a skit that tells your story and then act it out

* make an ad that tells your story

* write a song that tells the story and sing it as a group

* make pictures that show the story of what you did

* make hand puppets and use them to tell your story

* make a video that tells your story

* make up a game that tells your story

* create an exhibit or a set of booths that tells your story

Your Place in the World of Girls!

The world is filled with so many girls and so many stories. Now, how about telling a story full of action, surprise, adventure, and fun—a story all about you and your place in the world of girls!

Express Your BEST!

There are many ways to tell your story. Write down what you like to do and see what ideas you come up with! If you like to draw, paint, or doodle, you might make a painting, draw a self-portrait, or create a cartoon story. If you play a musical instrument or love to sing, you might tell your story with a song, or by singing songs that your friends write. If you like to act or make up voices and tell jokes, maybe you'll perform in a play or give a speech.

Whatever you choose, be sure to show your audience how much it means to you to make a positive change in the world!

Your STRENGTHS  and TALENTS

You have so many strengths and talents. Think of all the things that have made you proud on this journey.

Ask the women in your life to tell you at least one strength or talent they see in you. You might talk to your mother, your aunts, your grandmothers, your sisters, or a trusted teacher or neighbor.

Strengths and Talents I Have

_____

_____

_____

Strengths and Talents That Women in My Life See in Me

_____

_____

_____

What I like to do:

_____

_____

_____

_____

How I can use what I like to do to tell my story:

_____

_____

_____

_____

QUILTS THAT TELL STORIES

Faith Ringgold makes quilts that tell stories. "My ideas come from thinking about my life," Faith says.

One of her quilts is called "Tar Beach." It tells a story from Faith's childhood of hot summer nights, when her father would put a mattress on the tar roof of their apartment building in New York City. Her mother would spread a sheet and put pillows on top of the mattress. Then Faith, her brother and sister and parents would lie down together on the roof to cool off. From so high up, they could see lots of tall buildings and the George Washington Bridge.

In her story quilt, an 8-year-old girl dreams of owning the tall buildings and the bridge, and helping her parents have a better life. Faith made her story of Tar Beach into a book, too.

Faith made her first painted quilt with her mother, Willi Posey, who taught her how to sew.

So Many Ways to MAKE ART

Look around you. The women in your world express themselves in many ways. They might sew, draw, or write poetry. What can you learn from them? And how can you take what you learn and add something to it to make it your own?

COMBINE Your Talents!

Sometimes it's hard to choose just one way to express yourself. Well, you don't have to! You could add fabric to a painting, like Faith Ringgold did. You could dance and sing. You could decorate the inside and outside of a box to make a little room that tells your story.

Ask yourself: How can I best show my place in the world of girls? Look back at your "Express Your Best" list on page 32 to decide!

Girls in the WORLD, Girls in YOUR WORLD!

New York City is much bigger these days than when Faith Ringgold was a girl. Around 4 million girls and women live there now. In all the United States, there are more than 150 million women and girls!

Just for fun, count how many girls and women you see in one day. Keep count here.

Congratulations! YOU Have a STORY to Tell!

You've explored the wide world of girls and how you fit in it. You've heard lots of stories, found lots of clues, and used those clues to think about important changes in the world!

As you keep going in Girl Scouts, you'll hear many more stories and many more clues. The world is filled with stories, and those stories keep the world turning, 'round and 'round!

One story you can always tell is the story of this journey. Give it a try!

The story of this journey is

_____

_____

_____

_____

_____

Remember, Your Story Is JUST BEGINNING . . .

A story begins, has a middle and end,
with people or creatures
who may become friends.

There's a place where things happen,
a mood dark or light,
a sunshiny day or a cool moonlit night.

As you read, you may tingle
and think you are there.
You may see, hear, and feel things.
Good books make you care.

You've read many stories
and heard many told.
Your favorites are stories
that never grow old.

So your turn has come.
Tell your story, please do!
It's a wonderful tale of
the leader who is you!

A WORLD of GIRLS! How Do You Say GIRL in FRENCH?

DO YOU KNOW? WRITE IT HERE!

My PASSPORT Tells a Great STORY

You've seen that stories can give you ideas for what needs to change for the better. And you know that making those changes is a way to improve things for girls all over the world. You're always on the lookout for how to make the world better. That's the story of being a Girl Scout!

Hear a Story

To earn the Hear a Story award, search your memory, you library, your favorite movies, TV shows, and books for one really great story that has a clue in it about something that needs to change.

The story you read or hear can be old or new. It can take place near you or far, far away. It can be from a storybook or something that really happened. But the story you choose has something in it that needs to change—something you can make better in the world.

The story I found was _____.

This story is about _____.

In this story, _____ *needs to change.*

By changing _____, *the world for girls*

will be better because _____.

In my world, I could change this, too, by _____

_____.

Change a Story

To earn the Change a Story award, you and your Brownie team act on a clue in a story, to change things for the better for girls in your world.

The story we chose together was _____

_____ .

The clue in the story was _____ .

The change we decided to make for girls in our community was _____

_____ .

Tell a Story

To earn the Tell a Story award, you and your Brownie team describe to others how you heard a clue in a story and then changed the story for the better for girls in your own world.

My Brownie team talked about the best audience to hear our story. We decided our audience should be_____

_____

because _____

_____ .

We told our **World of Girls** story to this audience.

We explained that we are sharing our story to inspire others to keep the change going strong!

BETTER WORLD
for Girls!

These are some of the feelings I have when I think about being part of a world of girls:

_____

_____ .

I created a work of art to show what it means to me to be part of a world of girls.

I gave it this title: _____ .

I showed it to: _____

_____ .

This is how I would describe my work of art:

_____

_____

_____

_____

_____

_____

_____

_____

_____

_____ .

The BROWNIE FRIENDS' Passport

Alejandra, Campbell, and Jamila traveled to:

_____

_____

_____

They found these **clues**:

_____

_____

They decided to make these things **better**:

_____

_____

They decided to tell their **new stories** by:

_____

_____

Where I would like to see the Brownie friends **travel next**:

_____

_____

Give Your Book a FLIP!

See what fun you'll have on the other side as you find stories, share stories, and change stories!